T0114708

HANNAH'S OTHER BOOKS ARE:

"Altars of Remembrance"

"More altars of remembrance"

"Endless altars of remembrance"

"New Wine"

UNWORTHY, BUT ACCEPTED

We never stop learning and passing it on

HANNAH HOFER

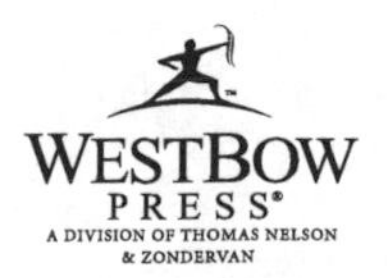

Copyright © 2023 Hannah Hofer.

All rights reserved. No part of this book may be used or reproduced by any means, graphic, electronic, or mechanical, including photocopying, recording, taping or by any information storage retrieval system without the written permission of the author except in the case of brief quotations embodied in critical articles and reviews.

WestBow Press books may be ordered through booksellers or by contacting:

WestBow Press
A Division of Thomas Nelson & Zondervan
1663 Liberty Drive
Bloomington, IN 47403
www.westbowpress.com
844-714-3454

Because of the dynamic nature of the Internet, any web addresses or links contained in this book may have changed since publication and may no longer be valid. The views expressed in this work are solely those of the author and do not necessarily reflect the views of the publisher, and the publisher hereby disclaims any responsibility for them.

Any people depicted in stock imagery provided by Getty Images are models, and such images are being used for illustrative purposes only.
Certain stock imagery © Getty Images.

Scripture quotations are taken from the New King James Version®. Copyright © 1982 by Thomas Nelson. Used by permission. All rights reserved.

ISBN: 978-1-6642-9182-9 (sc)
ISBN: 978-1-6642-9183-6 (e)

Print information available on the last page.

WestBow Press rev. date: 02/08/2023

CONTENTS

THIS CONTINUES THE STORIES OF GOD'S FAITHFULNESS

How amazing, I would have never imagined writing a book, much less five of them. This shows me that it is wise to be aware of the leading of this awesome God. As He says in Psalm 32:8 which promises "I will instruct you and teach you in the way you should go, I will guide you with My eye on you." This must have been the scripture I claimed second most, especially while raising my four children alone and the hundreds of students the Lord gave me to teach every week.

The number one scripture I love is that the word which goes forth from His mouth will not return to Him without doing what He sent it for, in Isaiah 55:11. He says, "So shall My word be that goes forth from My mouth, it shall not return to Me void, but it shall accomplish what I please, and it shall prosper in the thing for which I sent it."

I claimed this daily over my children, asking Him to let their knowledge of Himself be accomplished as My Savior pleases. This I prayed for my children, grandchildren and my so far 25 great grandchildren daily, trusting Him to do as He has promised. The thing I have seen to be one of God's character traits is that He is totally trustworthy.

Knowing that this Word is sent for Salvation gives me real confidence when I witness about His faithfulness. Having been a voluntary Bible teacher in the city's Youth Detention Center for 35 years, shows His word to truly change lives as this faithful God draws these teenagers to Himself.

There were many comments from the staff, that the attitudes of the young prisoners changed after they had attended the Bible studies. My not being allowed to see them on the outside unless being ordained, I began 1-1/2 years of schooling and after graduating, Campus Crusade for Christ had me ordained.

This began a new kind of ministry and my beloved Savior protected me from any kind of danger. They were not allowed to know where I live, so I usually picked them up and we spend the day at the beach, in the mountains or in a church office. This provided special times of prayers, which were not possible when in a group because the young men were more relaxed. Of the 41 Units of 22 youths each were all young men. There were only two Units of girls, and they chose to have male teachers.

The ministry at the Youth Detention Center continued when I followed my job and moved to San Clemente, in Orange County, for ten years. The distance to the Juvenile Detention Center was much further than my city before, but my Lord had special reasons for this also. Due to one of my grandsons joining the Marines, I had the chance to start Bible studies on Camp Pendleton Marine Base in Orange County, California. These studies were three days a week, for three hours each night.

FAITHFULNESS IN LITTLE BRINGS MORE

Having been faithful in my ministries, and by the financial help of my faithful supporters, the new one to the Marines became my favorite of Bible teachings. One of the reasons was because those of my Bible students who were off for the weekend were allowed to come to my home. This meant they did not have to go to the city with the other Marines, and they were very grateful because the temptations there were great.

I love my pictures on the weekends of seven high-school graduates that are now Marines, on the weekends, wrapped in sleeping bags on my living room floor. These are, according to which company is back on Base. After breakfast we spent time in prayer, at the beach and on Sundays at my church. There were some very meaningful and blessed situations that are unforgettable. I stayed in touch with some after they left to go to their next assignments.

One young Marine got notice that his father was killed and after returning back to the Base, he hugged me and said I was the only one he could talk to besides God. We had some healing and comforting prayer times. All my young soldiers called me Mom and I know I shared this in my first book, but it helped in missing my two daughters, my two sons and my grand babies. Finally, I got it worked out where I spent one weekend with my children and one with my Marines.

After graduating my young soldiers had to leave for their permanent stations. They all left me precious letters, thanking God for having me there for them. I still have all those letters and when Satan tries to discourage me, I read them to him, and he departs. The reason this became the favorite of my ministries is because these students I was allowed to see outside of the Base.

CONTINUING THESE BLESSED ADVENTURES

My precious 45 years with Campus Crusade for Christ, since June 8th,1977, have been a time of growing and chances to be a blessing to others. Asking myself if I am still receiving and accepting His Grace when I fail, makes me search more in that precious Word of God. I never forget the day I gave my life to the Savior and began to read the first Bible I ever had.

Being able to travel overseas when my daughters were married and my sons had joined the Service, was an awesome gift. It truly broadened my vision of God's amazing love for those He had died for to save. There being no limit to His love, made me trust in His plan for my life. This greatly limited my fear of the enemy, so off I went. The most unusual and risky mission trips were to the rural areas of India and one I will share about Aman in Jordan.

The roads to these villages in India, were small and ruff and could only be traveled by foot but we loaded the biggest equipment on the motorized tricycles. The results were amazing because almost all of the villager's prayed the Salvation prayer, and we had volunteers to do follow up Bible studies with them. It was such a blessing to see the earnestness of these precious new believers. All of them wanted a greater knowledge of this God, who said that He loves them.

One village only had electricity at their Temple, but the elders allowed us to plug our generator in right behind their god, which was a big black cow. They had fastened our screen right in front of the cow and above and besides were more of the gods. Since it was night, we had to step into the cow dung because the cows were part of the audience. We were not allowed to chase them away because they were holy. In each of the villages the results were such a blessing and they wanted to know more about this Jesus.

THE MOST AWESOME SHOWING OF ALL

One of the film showings was in Jordan, right on the Israel border, to refugees waiting for their Jordan-citizenship. There were supposed to be 35 who wanted to see the Jesus Film. So, my two partners and I took off. We kept driving lower and lower and it kept getting hotter and hotter, and I asked the driver if he knew where he was going.

He explained to me that we are going to the lowest part of Jordan, and we were now below water level. I was informed to get my passport ready at which I reacted in shock. I said, why my passport, we are in Jordan, and we are showing the film there? I did not bring my passport. They answered, we will be right on the Israeli border where we must go through three checkpoints of soldiers with rifles.

They went on to tell me that we must have passports and will have to get our bodies checked for guns while they search the car. Sending up a sincere prayer, I watched while one of those soldiers, with his rifle at the driver, said something to him. Suddenly the soldier looked at me, and to my partner's surprise, waved us to drive on.

My two companions, in total surprise explained that this had never happened before, there had always been a total search.

Well, the other two checkpoints came up and while we were praising our God, the soldiers also looked in and waved us through. This proved to us that this protecting Lord knew exactly our location and had already worked out our safety. When we arrived, instead of the 35 who scheduled for the showing, there arrived 112, and almost all prayed the payer of Salvation.

I still have the video and the pictures of that film showing and enjoy it when I share it with someone. They loved being prayed for after the movie and my interpreter and I were done way after midnight. Someone was telling us of a way to get back to Aman a different way, it was about half an hour longer, but it had no checkpoints. My two partners and I sang praise songs to our God all the way home.

HIS SALVATION COMES IN SO MANY WAYS

A different type of adventures were my daily prayers for my four children, my eight grandchildren, 25 great grandchildren and all those in-laws having joined our family. It is a challenge for this 84-year-old lady remembering their names and birthdays. Not wanting them left behind when Jesus comes for His own, I started Bible studies at Grandpa's house, there were usually eleven or twelve young people. They came faithfully and sometimes brought friends.

Having been with accounting in the first five years when the Lord called me to Campus Crusade for Christ was a real challenge. When I ask the Lord for a more spiritual work, He had me switched to the Donor Development Department. This is a part of the Jesus Film Project I have worked with for 41 years now and truly came to love it.

This film, inspired by Jesus Christ and created by Campus Crusade for Christ, now called CRU, has been in every country of the world since its creation. It exists in more than 2,000 languages and has been filmed completely in the Holy Land. It is made entirely after the Gospel of Luke, which the viewers receive a copy of at the end of the performances.

This beloved God has allowed me 63 trips to 29 countries, many countries more than once. While at home, the Lord used me by teaching the Bible in four city schools. My daytime job was five days a week with Campus Crusade, where I informed our donors what God is doing all over the world. This meant I received the latest reports from our ministries being done and it kept my spirit high. It gave me great joy to pass on His precious work being completed in all these countries.

However, my Savior drew me into four personal ministries as well, which my faithful supporters made possible for us to achieve. The first one was powerful Bible studies to the city's Youth Detention Center, called Juvenile Hall. The Lord turned this into 35 years of leading tens of thousands of young prisoners into the arms of a loving God, who never tired of bringing them closer to Himself. My heart and mind were strongly on my Bible studies being only from the Word.

Having been saved by God, three years after my husband had left our four children and me, began an unimaginable, adventurous life for us. It was at the lowest part of my life and came by a lady from Campus Crusade for Christ and was a total God plan. Not only was I not looking for God but having heard about Him made me hide in fear rather than seek Him.

This is why this Salvation is so miraculous because no one else but God could have come up with this. He has an awesome imagination. Planning to go and sell makeup, on a hot July day, was not wise. At my first door a young lady answered and said she had just moved here. She introduced herself, and her being on staff with a big mission agency was no coincident. Besides her leading me to a God who would forgive everything I have ever done wrong, made us totally forget about the makeup.

My being on foot was because my oldest daughter and her friends had snugged my keys and car, and totaled it without any injuries to them. The other amazing part of it was that this sweet spiritual sister had just moved there, and I was the first chance she had to witness Salvation to anyone. But there is something even more amazing about this Salvation.

She asked if she could read me from a little yellow booklet and since she had been so kind to me, I agreed. Not only did what she read made sense to me, but I was totally attracted by it. When we got to the prayer in the booklet, I began to weep and deeply desired what it said. Longing to be forgiven by this mighty God of love, I also wanted to be loved again.

Since my ex-husband had passed away in his 4th year of being absent from us, I needed to find a job. Even though my two little sons having to go to childcare was hard on me, but this newly found God began to show His faithfulness. Not only did He provide a job for me at Campus Crusade for Christ but made the time with my boys special in our new church.

CONTINUED GROWTH AND FALLING IN LOVE

Some wonderful classes and speakers were made available at Campus Crusade, and I just could not get enough of the teachings. A spiritual advisor offered my girls and me Bible lessons as well and our church had added a Christian movie night each week. I enjoyed starting my boys in the knowledge of this awesome God which was also a part of my growing deeper in love with Him.

Witnessing was scary in the beginning but once I experienced the wonderful satisfaction of the Savior having taken someone else away from Satan, I wanted more. Campus Crusade and my church gave me plenty of that opportunity of witnessing and I could thank my Savior for having chosen me as His own. Of course, I started first of all with my own family and friends, they could not be left behind.

Realizing from the Scriptures that the Lord has me here now, knowing He can use me at this troubled time, caused me to be confident, not worried. I just needed to trust Him more than ever before and to let Him do His work without interfering. Entering my life, He gave me a measure of faith, according to Romans 12:3, which helped me to believe what He promised.

What made this new faith so amazing was that what was taught me seemed so real. There was no doubt or questioning about what the Bible was presenting, I accepted it as reality. As it says in Psalm 136:1 – 26, about His mercy enduring forever and the praises just continue, it amazed me that there were no doubts in my mind about any of the scriptures being real. This had to be His gift.

Never having heard these things before, especially this great and unconditional love He has for the children He gave His life for, just drew my heart to Him. The Holy Spirit showed me that this faith and my obedience is how He was able to use me and draw so many to Himself. It made my desire to be a vessel for Him to use, even stronger.

I have to believe and study His word because knowledge does not come instantly, and I have to protect what I am being taught so the enemy cannot snatch it away. Some interaction with my God and His word, will be a joy to me and all I am going to teach it to. A planted seed takes continued feeding and watering to be strong and growing, it is the same with the word of God.

THE BEAUTIFUL EXAMPLES FROM THE OLD TESTAMENT

Especially in my many overseas trips, the longing of God to reach these nations became real to me, as I saw their longing to know more about Him. That is why the fascination with so many of the Old Testament stories were a joy for me to teach to the about 300 youths a week now. I especially love the account of the chariots in the sky.

My favorite one is in 2 Kings 6:16 -17 where the king of Syria sent a great army to Dothan to capture Elisha. When his servant got scared, Elisha said "Do not fear, for those who are with us are more than those who are with them." And Elisha prayed and said "Lord I pray, open his eyes that he may see. Then the Lord opened the eyes of the young man and he saw. And behold the mountains were full of horses and chariots of fire all around Elisha's home."

This reminds me of Matthew 26:53 where Jesus says to Peter after he cut off the soldier's ear, "Or do you think that I cannot now pray to My Father, and He will provide Me with twelve legions of angels?" I googled it and one legion is 6,000, this means x12 is 72,000 angles on chariots. Wow, I can just imagine these stories and try to picture them which reveals to me even more of the greatness of my God. I cannot wait to see Him face to face and worship Him for all eternity.

The promises of the Lord are mostly unconditional, so my attention is on the conditional ones. Like in 2 Chronicles 7:14 "if My people who are called by My name will humble themselves and pray and seek My face and turn from their wicked ways, then I will hear from heaven, and will forgive their sin and heal their land."

WOW, there is no clearer and more direct promise to have our country healed than that. Neither can I imagine that we believers do not do everything possible to fulfill His request. My heart aches to make our Creator, who loves us so deep and constant, be happy with our land. Needing Him so desperately makes me long to use every moment to reach out to those who live without these promises He gives.

THESE AWESOME PROMISES INCREASE

Jesus said in John 14:12 “Most assuredly, I say to you, he who believes in Me, the works that I do he will do also, and greater works than these he will do, because I go to My Father.” Wow, that is such powerful encouragement to seek out and ask for true revelation. Can I really be that close to my Savior and be that much a part of Him? Oh, let it be!

Having realized in my 48 years with this awesome Creator that nothing is impossible with Him working miracles in my children, grandchildren and great grandchildren. I can surely vouch for His promises being real. Even my two grandchildren being with Him already and the nine who were lost in my family by miscarriage, and are waiting for me, makes me trust His plans completely .

Meeting them all, including seeing the family members I knew and nine unborn I have not met yet, makes heaven so much sweeter. Besides first seeing and hugging my beloved triune God, I can hardly wait to put my arms around all of them. Those beautiful scriptures about our awesome future gives me so much joy and hope that nothing here can depress or discourage me.

The powerful word in Romans 8:38 and 39 are often on my mind and I love teaching them: "For I am persuaded that neither death nor life, not angels nor demons nor powers, nor things present nor things to come, nor height nor depth, nor any other created thing, shall be able to separate us from the love of God which is in Christ Jesus our Lord."

This is obviously a very powerful life changing scripture because it says that nothing and no one can take me away from this loving saving God. This means I have absolutely no excuse if my life is absent from Him. However, much worse, it also means that my eternity would be without Him also.

JESUS CLAIMS TO BE THE TRUTH

These warnings and promises are what His precious word, the Bible, is all about, there would no reason for me to reject Him. His children are the purpose this Savior God created the world in the first place and all He wants is to be loved back. This is my desire to do for the rest of my life here and then for all eternity.

He is either Lord of all in my life or He is not Lord at all to me. I do not desire a halfway relationship with this God who gave me His all. No temporary or partial following, His awesome Grace is given undeserved and cannot in any way be earned. My Savior did not give me a partial forgiveness of sins but a total one, and a forever washing away of them.

He who started His precious work in me promised to finish it and that is because His love is unlimited. He had given me an assignment and like He finished His assignment of Salvation, so I desire to finish mine. I love how this God stated in Psalm 33:9 and 11 where it says that "He spoke and it was done, He commanded, and it stood fast." And in verse 11 "The counsel of the Lord stands forever, the plans of His heart to all generations."

How can anyone doubt or question this Creator's honesty, why would He deceive us after all He went through. Deception is only the enemy's tactic and his favorite dirty game to play. This was something I made my children aware off from the beginning. It was important to me that they not only knew the greatness of their God, but also the wickedness of their enemy.

When I began the ministry my God had called me to, it was so important that my knowledge of the truth was very real. It tells us in James 3:1 "let not many of you become teachers, knowing that we shall receive a stricter judgement." This why, when it seemed that this is what He wanted me to be, I kept on searching the scriptures for His truth.

GOD'S WORK IS MEANINGFUL AND LASTING

The first spiritual work my Lord led me to was in the city's Juvenile Detention Center with troubled youths. The last thing these precious young people needed was someone else to deceive them and tell them lies. It was a true blessing to see their Savior draw one after another into His arms and help each to believe in His love for them.

That enabled me to take His love for me more real and made me long to share all this truth with my beloved students. These youths loved to be prayed for and seriously prayed for their family members. Many of them had girlfriends on the outside and a few even already were fathers, so the young men's prayers for them were sincere and from the heart.

Hearing the stories about their young lives made me grateful that my own children did not experience any abuse at home. Even though their earthly father was absent, their heavenly Father was invited to take over, and so He did. My prayers for my Juvenile

Hall kids were daily and from my heart and this awesome Savior intervened where He was allowed to.

The Sunday morning services I was allowed to give, at this Detention Center were really special, and almost everyone attended. Only the one or two on lock-down were not released for the service.

The prayers for my own children, grandchildren and the twenty-fife great grandchildren, as well as my first great great grandchild and my in-laws are daily. I love this because it makes me a part of their lives. The changes and improvements our God brought about were amazing and a true blessing. It was a joy to me when I heard them thank God for improvements and gifts.

My beloved God knows them because they received His son, of my prayers daily, and my reminding Him to give them wisdom and the ability to judge good from evil. As it has been my longing to honor this awesome Creator, it is my continued hope that they will also. By them being always a part of my life, lifting them up before their Savior gives meaning to my life.

In never letting them be an idol or stumbling block in my life, allows me to live in that beautiful rest my Lord talks about. God has made them all a part of my learning and growing. Just as with Martha at her brother's death and in her pain, she still acknowledged Jesus as God. He told her in John 11:25 "I am the resurrection and the life."

HE COMES ONLY AS FAR AS HE IS WANTED

This precious Savior never forces Himself on anyone, the desire for Him must be real and longing, only then will He move. Not only in times of trials or loss did I run to Him for help, so seeking His presence finally became a habit. All His times of faithfulness helped me to believe my Saviors reports and instantly reject the lies of the enemy.

The first promise which was my joy to pass on to my now about 190 Bible students a week was Isaiah 43:1-7 which begins with: "Fear not, for I have redeemed you (by the blood of My son) I have called you by your name (Christian), you are Mine. :2 When you pass through the waters, I will be with you and through the rivers, they shall not overflow you, you are Mine."

This is such an awesome promise that I am His, I keep saying and reminding myself often. The enemy tried to convince me that this was written only for Israel, until I came to verse :7 which says, "Everyone who is called by My name, whom I have created for My glory, I have formed him, yes, I have made him." This was so awesome to me and whenever trouble came into my life, I rested in these promises.

It continues in verse :21 "This people I have formed for Myself, they shall declare My praise." There was always real comfort and assurance with my students that God considers them "His" and that they can declare His praise. Many of these young people said that they want to do better in their lives and declare His praise from now on.

What a joy their desires must have been to their Savior, and I feel sure they had His help and strength in this. Even the staff at Juvenile Hall admitted that many who attended Bible study had better attitudes. These were allowed to come out and visit with me on visiting day Sunday afternoon, when no one came to see them.

A GREAT EXAMPLE IN DANIEL CHAPTER THREE

Only my God knows my future and He will reveal it to me as He finds it is needed. This is how He can be sure that I will not interfere. I have been known to run ahead of His plan and I had to repent and wait on His timing. In Daniel chapter three, where it tells the story of the three Hebrew youths who were thrown into the fire for their commitment to God.

Their faithful honoring of their God was rewarded, and they did not have to bow down to anyone else. The Lord allowed them to be greatly tempted with the best this foreign country had to offer. However, their unwavering steady trust brought the favor of God to them in front of these unbelievers.

Learning early in my Christian life that friendship with the world is enmity with God, so, my old life had to be left behind. At first it seemed almost impossible, but by the Grace of God, one step at the time, is bringing the separation about. Gratefully I acknowledge a longtime bad habit has bitten the dust and a new idea replaced it.

This wonderful God has always heard my prayers and answered at His perfect timing. Sometimes His answer lasted along with many lessons to be learned in between time, my Lord always answered the way it was best for me. Sharing the hardest and longest one with you, I pray will give hope and encouragement to you.

This is about my beloved youngest daughter Christina, who has kept me most of all in touch with our God. Having shared it shortly before, I will extend a little more. She had always been very close to her Daddy and his leaving was especially painful to her. Every broken promise of picking her up and not showing, left a new bruise on her heart.

My being the only one there to be blamed, brought about a very unhappy relationship under which we both suffered many years. But God, in His great love and with needed lessons brought about His answer. So, the blessed day came when Christina put her arms around me and said I love you mom and we hugged and cried, knowing it was God's gift.

It showed many of our family members and friends never to stop their prayers, the answer always comes in the Father's way and time. Both of us being blessed, we enjoyed sharing things we were not free to before, and we were thanking our Lord daily. It finally made our lives what our Creator had meant for them to be, and it pleased Him and us.

MORE ABOUT THE POWER OF PRAYER

There were many painful and lonely times in my life, however after my Savior entered, these became less and finally stopped. This awesome Creator held me in His loving arms and saw me through these times as soon as they hit my conciseness. This has enabled me to teach His precious word with assured confidence.

Scriptures like Psalm 18:1-3 helped me greatly to respond back to this God of love. "Lord You are my rock and my fortress and my deliverer, my God, my strength, in you I will trust, my shield and the horn of my Salvation, my stronghold," and verse :3 "I will call upon You Lord, You are worthy to be praised, so shall I be saved from my enemies."

This shows why David was called a man after God's own heart, not because he was without fault, but because he truly knew his Creator. He also knew how to pray and how to confess his sins and repent. That is why I brought my failures quickly to my Savior, keeping them on me would have given my enemy an open door into my heart.

Being simply human is not a negative to me because my heartfelt prayer is daily to be some day completely in the image of my God. The Bible promises that when I see Him face to face, I will be like Him. This is awesome and the waiting time is short if He uses me in the harvest of those searching for His love and peace.

Believing that my God has a great future for me helps me to be aware of His presence and listening for His voice. That is why my conversations with Him are often like prayer, especially when I talk with Him about people that need Him. He only goes where He is invited, so, my first thought and attention in the morning is on Him which blesses my day.

TEACHING HIS WORD ALWAYS

Whenever God changes the heart, it also changes the behavior. His word tells us clearly in James 4:1 and 3, "where do wars and fights come from among you? Do they not come from your desires for pleasure that war in your members?" and in :3 "You ask and do not receive, because you ask amiss, that you may spend it on your pleasures."

Wow, that started a brand-new chapter in my life because I could totally relate to this rebuke. This was something that had to be healed in my children's and my life and so I went to prayer. The teaching in 1John 5:15 brought real comfort because it says, "And if I know that He hears me, whatever I ask, I know that I have the petitions."

This was such a help and made me take praying to God very seriously. Teaching on that subject brought my student's attention also, since I presented it as a problem with myself not with them. They could see that wrong desires were common, even to Christians, which made it easier for them to be honest with their Savior about them.

Understanding that God hears their prayers made them more aware about being respectful and not flippant. Our prayer times became more serious and meaningful, awaiting the answers to them became more patiently. Together we saw that our Savior kept His promise about answering them, even if not at our way or timing.

Relating to these young people that God knows their future, helped them, as it had for me, to really consider the choices for prayer. It helped to think if this was really what they wanted. It was a great lesson for all of us since this faithful God promised to give what we asked for. We also learned together that His delays always have a purpose.

Especially their court times kept them often in stress. Whenever their planned time in court came up, the decision was revealed when they would be released. If it was the time for any of them to go home, one of the family members had to sign for them. When there was no one there to sign, they had to return to their cell.

It was hard for me to convince them that it was not the Lord's perfect timing for them yet. Helping them to realize that this may be a wrong time for them to be out and it may not be safe till next court session, was not easy. Many had to wait till someone from the family picked them up, but they still came and attended Bible study and prayer time.

THEIR SINS AND LAWLESS DEEDS I WILL REMEMBER NO MORE

There are promises in the Old and the New Testament that have always brought tears to my eyes. They show clearly the deep and unconditional love and mercy of our God. One of these beautiful statements is in Hebrews 10:17, where He states, "Their sins and their lawless deeds I will remember no more."

It revealed to me and all believers that at judgement day, He is not going to bring out our past failures and mistakes. When I first read this, over and over, it made me realize that there was a chance for me to go to heaven. There was such a relieve and joy and I began to fall more in love with this awesome God.

This love has of course deepened and grown stronger with every new revelation of this Creator and Savior. Since I could never recall all His precious works and miracles in my life, I will just gratefully thank Him daily and forever. Having experienced His love and mercy since July of 1974, I can only share what I can remember.

By recalling my Salvation Day makes my heart rejoice because I can almost feel the depression in my heart and mind on the way to sell some makeup. However, there was peace and a real relieve after the Salvation prayer. With my background and the pain of rejection, I had finally found a hope for my future.

When the Bible tells me in Ephesians 1:4-5, that this awesome God has known me before He made the world, overwhelms me. After that He had to wait till I was 37 years old before I gave my heart and life to Him. This kind of patience is something I pray for because it would surely improve my life.

HE DID NOT NEED ME BUT HE WANTED ME

My God had a purpose for me and only He knows the ending. When He chose me, He was aware of the times I would obey and the times I would go against His will. Yet since before He laid the foundations of the world my Savior had my days already written in His book. He tells me about these beautiful words in Psalm 139, that He has searched me and known me.

How could I not love back such an awesome One who created the world and me, knowing all the good and bad in advance. Even though my Lord comprehended my path and is acquainted with all my ways, He never once deserted me. He also says that there is not a word on my tongue that this amazing God not already knows.

When teaching this meaningful song of David, my students always paid full attention and had many questions and comments. Starting simply where I was and in my limited knowledge of the scriptures, my Creator had a plan for me. My request for Him to send me was approved and He provided what was needed to make me useful.

That is why it was so important that I did not copy my Christian brothers and sisters because He gave them their own assignments and talents. My beloved God has never allowed me to quit, but the harder it got, the closer I clung to Him. This made it easier for Him to plan, even around my mistakes and misunderstandings.

Putting on my God's powerful armor, I would take up the sword, which is His word, and stand. Being told to stand, I obeyed, because my Savior has already won the battle, and my enemies were defeated. This allowed me to keep my mind and my eyes on those who needed to know this wonderful God of love.

HIS WORD IS THE SWORD OF THE SPIRIT

By using that powerful word of God whenever the chance came up, not only lifted my spirit but protected me from Satan's lies. It is only possible for me to recognize his deceptions, if I know the truth. My sister was the manager in a bank and she told me the bank's tactic of teaching their new employees.

These new staff would learn how to handle and work with legal money all day. As soon as their superiors' snug in a counterfeit bill, they would instantly recognize it because they knew the real money. That is how we will begin to identify God's truth, by being much in the "love letter" He wrote to the children He loves so much.

It is just the same when the Savior calls me for a certain task, it is obvious that it can only be done because the needs have already been provided. This faithful God would never leave me stranded and exposed to the enemy. For that very reason, the protective armor of God has been given to me for daily use.

The awesome promises and encouragements from the One who has redeemed me, kept me from being intimidated or scared. Whenever my enemies tried to tell me I was to week to follow His command, I remembered that my Savior said that when I am week, He is strong. This kept me from fear and helped me to move ahead.

Being told to come to my God as I am, kept me from pretending to be someone I was not. It meant for me to come humbly without taking any credit for the good which had been done. The only way the call and the goal God had given me would be a blessing is if I acknowledge Who's work it really is.

GOD'S WORD HAS NEVER BEEN STOPPED

Finding out that the Bible has always been and still is the most sold book in the world brought me great joy. In 1455 a man called Johannes Gutenberg, in a city near my hometown, invented the printing press and the first thing he printed was the Bible. Being grateful that the Lord kept it well and used all these years, I am praying that He will much increase it.

The awesome instructions and guidance of God's love letter to His children has every subject in life covered. Therefore, it is so valuable to the Christians, there is no other book that can compare in wisdom and knowledge. My daily time in this precious letter has become my instructions for life and I am so thankful.

One thing it tells me which I am grateful for is, that Satan has to ask permission before he can harm me, and that Jesus will pray for me. Being exposed to that enemy would be so scary otherwise. My wanting to be like my perfect Savior draws me to His loving instructions and warnings, which are set before me to follow.

It gives me such great examples for making mistakes and for second chances. Peter's denying Jesus did not get him out of the Master using him. Even when Jesus asked to see the disciples, He especially mentioned Peter's name. This gives me great comfort when I mess up and after confession, wait to hear my beloved Savior's voice again.

When Peter apologizes for being so human, Jesus confirms that he will still be fishing for men. Even though Peter does not understand the real meaning of that yet, it becomes clear to him on Pentecost. Having the Holy Spirit in him then, gives Peter the knowledge and courage to speak on behalf of the Son of God, without any fear.

Jesus prayed that Peters faith would not fail and that, when he returns to Jesus, he should strengthen his brethren. Even when I made a mistake in my Christian walk, I did not allow Satan to pressure me with guilt. Instead, I looked for someone who was discouraged and needed help, so I could point him or her to the Savior.

IT'S NEVER A COINCIDENT

A great example is Esther's story, starting with the king not being able to sleep. Who but God could make him read the story of Mordecai in all those books. Esther's uncle was being honored and Esther had the courage to reveal her nationality to the king. As God planned, Haman was hung instead of Mordecai and the Jews got saved.

Her uncle Mordecai told her that she was chosen to be here for such a time as this. That said she was meant to save her people, the Jews, from being killed. Once she understood that this was her reason for being in the palace, Esther came up with a plan to save the Jews from being wiped out by their enemy Haman.

BE AWARE OF WHAT COMES OUT OF MY MOUTH

What I say or pray for can become a reality, so trying to be aware of what I say became very important to me. Sometimes, when I try to impress someone, I have said or promised something that would be impossible for me to fulfill. Also, in agreeing to do something that I would not be able to do, I had to lie to get out of it.

I needed to learn to watch carefully about what I say because as a teacher I need to have a stronger judgement. Another important lesson was to be careful of who I listened to because if it was not from God's word, I had to reject it. My greatest responsibility was to teach my students only what was the truth which is related to us from God.

My conscience is my warning system from my Savior. As said in James 3:1-2, not many of you should become teachers, for you know that we who teach will be judged with greater strictness." It was the Holy Spirit living in me Who helped to be sure my lessons came from the Bible and were not my opinions.

Teaching God's word was not my conscious choice, it was my Creator who led me that way. However, when I was aware of this, I tried hard to make my lessons from the Bible. Using scriptures to prove my points gave me the peace of mind of not leading anyone astray. It came from the Holy Spirit, or I would not teach it.

Another Scripture that was a terrible warning, was: Matthew 18:6 which says, "Whoever causes one of these little ones, who believe in Me to sin, it would be better for him if a millstone were hung around his neck, and he were drowned in the depth of the sea." This made me very careful that I chose my lessons from God's word.

This scared me so that I was almost afraid to teach, but my Lord kept carrying me on. This choice was my Heavenly Fathers, and soon it became my goal. Satan attacked in the beginning but when my Savior showed that it was His idea not mine, I relaxed. The Bible studies at the Youth Detention Center in San Bernardino, then in the city of Orange, and at the Pregnancy and Family Center, became my call.

ONLY JESUS CAN CAUSE ME TO FOLLOW

Under God's strict, yet loving guidance I was able to follow His call, how and where He had chosen. It was so awesome to me that my Savior could use someone like me. Being a new Christian, not fluent in His word, and never having witnessed to anyone I carefully chose what I taught. The only thing I was aware of was that I had a longing to know Him and to be used.

Being in His word more and more I began to recognize His voice and kept following it to the best of best of my ability. It began to pull down, a little at a time, what had to go from my life, and it build up my trust and my faith. Only my Lord knows where and how far this will go, but I can rest in Him and find out. It will be a true joy to share this with you as it happens until He says it is time to come home.

The Bible says in Psalm 46:1 that God is our refuge and strength a very present help in trouble. This is great truth and encouragement, and I can vouch this to be as it says. The time I was not picked up at the airport, the time I missed my flight connection and more, this faithful Lord was present and had already worked it out

There were situations in which the faith of our Jesus Film Team had to be used in order to finish a showing because Satan's opposition was strong. The witches and satanic priests in these villages had unholy powers. So, it was vital that we believed strongly what it tells us in 1John 4:4, that "greater is He who is in me than he who is in the world."

No damage was ever done to people, only to equipment and we always took more than 1 projector. The reason the enemy tried to stop the Jesus Film showings was because people who received Jesus as their Lord and Savior were in the hundreds or thousands. They all wanted to know this God better.

A TRUE STORY ABOUT HANNAH AND LIZ

My full first name is Hannelore, a popular name in Europe. However, the short for this name is Hanni and that was my name until I was 19 years. Well, when I met my husband, he did not like his Army buddies calling me Hanni so he used my middle name and called me Liz. My family and friends were ok with that, so for my 15 years of marriage, I was Liz.

My move to the USA in 1959, at the age of 21, with my husband and our six-month-old daughter was great. We left Bremerhaven on Christmas eve and arrived in New York harbor on a famous warship called The USS Darby, which was an adventure. I loved my new country soon and getting a book and tape, English became my language quickly.

Since my husband was from San Bernardino, that is where I ended up. One year after I arrived my mom and two sisters followed me to the USA. Being happily married my husband and I added three more children and all was well. It was in the 15th year that my husband wanted to be single again and left us.

In my pain and loneliness, I went out dancing with some single mom's witch I met at my children's school. Our oldest kids watched the younger ones and off we went hoping to find a husband, at least I was. However, I found out soon that the men in these places had just left their families and were not taking on a new wife especially one with four kids

There came a point where I was planning suicide, which was also the time when the merciful God of heaven brought an end to this painful existence. On a very hot day in July of 1974, I went to sell some makeup and knocked on my first door and the young woman asked me in, offering a cold glass of water.

She introduced herself as being on staff with Campus Crusade for Christ and she had just moved here. Telling her that I just lost my car and therefore lost my job and was on foot, she asked if would like to give my troubles to a God that loves me. Being desperate, I said yes, and this precious lady led me to the Lord. At this special time of Salvation, Liz became Hanni again and reading the Bible the lady had given me, I found there was a Hannah in there, so I added an ah to the end of my name.

WILL THE OLD SELF EVER BE GONE ?

Beginning to know the Father, Son and Holy Spirit, I spent more time in the book God had written to His believers. My full name is Hannelore, and is very popular where I was born, however the short name for it is Hanni. My husband Bill, being American, did not like his Army buddies calling me Hanni, so he switched to my middle name and called me Liz. So, for the 15 years of our marriage I was Liz.

Liz had a bad temper and often that temper came out when she was put down or criticized. When Bill died, four years after he had left our family, Liz became a Christian and I wanted my old name back. However, instead of Hanni, I chose Hannah for the short version. Loving the story of Hannah in the Bible and since I waited eight years for my first son, I related to the lady in the Bible.

Growing in the Lord, I began to love and serve this awesome Creator the best I could, however Liz was still in me. My beloved Savior had minimized my temper greatly, however, when Hannah was criticized and put down, Liz came out to defend her. The last time was recent with Hannah and her daughter Chris. Satan could not stand it that the two women were sisters in Christ but also had just become friends.

So, the enemy started a senseless disagreement and when Chris criticized Hannah, out came Liz. In her bad temper, Hannah called her daughter a pig and the fight was on. This made absolutely no sense because Chris is a very clean person, but that is all Liz could come up with in her bruised ego. I begged our heavenly Father many times daily to help us make it right.

Thanks be to our God, both women, my daughter Chris and I, had approached Him and in His usual faithfulness, He dissolved the problem, and they made up. I had told Satan to get out of our lives and out of the house in Jesus' name, that he is a defeated enemy and Chris and I are both covered by the blood of our Savior Jesus Christ. Asking the Holy Spirit to fill us with His power and love, God took over and healed the situation.

BEING SENT TO FIND AND REACH THE LOST

When Jesus saved me, He chose me, knowing all He could do through me, because I was so willing to be used. The Savior was aware that there would not be perfection until I would have my new eternal body. So, He is going to work with me and in me until that wonderful day arrives. In the meantime, He knew I would be a pliable object, willing to obey Him.

The God I worship is the supreme ruler, faithful and trustworthy. He will not ask me to me to do anything He has not already equipped me for. One of the hard things was climbing up five flights of stairs where I lived in Jerusalem. I lived with a Campus Crusade staff family and the old building had no elevator.

There were so many times when it was planned for our team of four to show the Jesus Film in villages far from the cities, especially in India. Our Jeep could only drive so far before the road became too narrow and too rough to drive it. So, we loaded the film equipment on an electric tricycle, and we had to walk through the forest.

It was always worth it because almost all of the villagers prayed to receive Jesus Christ as Savior and Lord and wanted Bible studies. There was each time some Christian Nationals who already volunteered to follow up and teach these new believers. Their desire to know more about this loving God and His Son, their Savior, was such a blessing to us.

This kept us always willing and ready to go again the following day. Only Sunday was kept as a day of worship and fellowship. If there was a day, we could not show the film, the Campus Crusade national staff would take us on a bus for sightseeing. We were able to take pictures for the letters to our supporters which had sent us for this ministry.

HOW SHALL THEY PREACH

Often, I teach and use the precious words from Romans 10:13-15 which says: "For whoever calls on the name of the Lord shall be saved. How then shall they call on Him in whom they have not believed? And how shall they believe in Him of whom they have not heard? And how shall they hear without a preacher?

And how shall they preach unless they are sent? As it is written, 'How beautiful are the feet of those who preach the gospel of peace, who bring glad tidings of good things!" That is why I thank my precious supporters often for sending me to reach those, whom the Lord knew would become His children. Their willingness to know this God must be a true joy to Him.

What a great privilege to be used by this awesome Savior to go, after He had saved me so graciously! There will never be a way to thank Him enough for His wonderful plan of Salvation. Of course, I have all of eternity to thank Him, and that is what my plan is. In the meantime, I get to tell as many as possible that this is His plan for them also.

It is so assuring for me to read, that what He says cannot be changed, because He Himself never changes. I can claim this in Psalm 33:9 which tells me "For He spoke and it was done, He commanded and it stood fast." And in verse :11 "The counsel of the Lord stands forever, the plans of His heart to all generations."

God's word reveals also in Psalms 111:7 and 8, "The works of His hands are verity and justice. All His precepts (rules) are sure, they stand fast forever and ever and are done in truth and uprightness. With these and so many other promises like them, I would never dare to doubt this mighty and powerful Creator.

OUR GREAT GOD DOES RELENT

God's word tells us in Joel 2:13-14, "So rend your heart and not your garments, return to the Lord your God, for He is gracious and merciful, Slow to anger and of great kindness, and He relents from doing harm. Who knows if He will turn and relent and leave a blessing behind Him." I googled the word relent and it has so many meanings, so I will give the most common "give up, come around, give in, comply, let up, to soften."

I just love that scripture It tells me in His word that He never changes, however He is known to change His mind which is called "relent". One time I am aware of is in Jonah 3:10 "Then God saw their works, that they turned from their evil way, and God relented from the disaster that He had said He would bring upon them, and He did not do it."

Another time was with Moses, when God was going to destroy the people, but Moses prayed for them, and God relented and did not do it. Our Creator is merciful and always compassionate, and His children's prayers are a powerful tool in His sight. However, He tells us that without faith it is impossible to please Him, so this is most important.

elieveThis is what my Lord says very clearly in Hebrews 11:6 for he who comes to Him must believe that He is, and that He is a rewarder of those who diligently (steady and earnest) seek Him. It then gives me an example of all those who have been so faithful to their God and believed all He promised. That is why I, having the Holy Spirit in me, have no excuse not to believe .

Knowing for sure that my God is in me, I feel it is useless to ask Him for more of Him. Instead, bringing out what my precious Savior has already told me in His book is the beneficial thing to do. Believing His awesome promises and the strong warnings, have and will, encourage me to live this Christian life and learn to please Him.

ALL HAPPENS AT HIS TIME AN IN HIS WAY

If I would ask for double like Elisha did, I think that it would cause me to mess it up or I become very prideful. Since my God says in Proverbs 3:34 that He resists the proud but gives grace to the humble, and He says this three times, humility is my choice. Diligently seeking my Lord has been a great joy to me and I long to increase it.

Considering my Father's words in Colossians 2:6, He firmly says: "As you therefore have received Christ Jesus the Lord, so walk in Him, verse :10 "and you are complete in Him, who is the head of all principality and power. This so beautifully agrees with Romans 8:38 claiming that not even principalities can separate me from His love.

This is fascinating to me where it says in 1Cor 2:9 "Eye has not seen, nor ear heard, nor have entered into the heart of man the things which God has prepared for those who love Him." And then He says in verse :10 "But God has revealed them to us through His Spirit," and in verse :11 "no one knows the things of God except the Spirit of God."

It continues so beautifully in verse :12, "Now we have received, not the spirit of the world, but the Spirit who is from God, that we might know the things that have been freely given to us by God." These promises are so awesome to me that things that are not available to non-believers, have been revealed to His children by the Holy Spirit.

HIS MERCY IS NEVER ENDING

Isaiah 30:18 tells me "Therefore the Lord will wait, that He may be gracious to you, that He may have mercy on you. For the Lord is a God of Justice, blessed are those who wait for Him." The one thing the Lord has taught me most is waiting; this is why I love and desire the promises given to those who wait on the Lord.

Then in Psalms 27:14 it declares "wait for the Lord, be strong and take heart and wait for the Lord." Again, in Psalms 37:7, "Rest in the Lord and wait patiently for Him" and it continues in Psalm 37:9...but those who wait on the Lord, they shall inherit the earth. The word wait means hope, trust, anticipate, depend on.

My favorite however is Psalm 40:31 which teaches us "But those who wait on the Lord shall renew their strength, they shall mount up with wings like eagles, they shall run and not be weary, they shall walk and not faint." Having always been impatient, this was very important for me to turn away from and be an example to the young people.

In my dozens of overseas ministries, it was so vital to be patient and wait because there were hardly any times that something did not go wrong. Twice we got to our assigned country and were denied entrance. However, we knew how to defeat Satan by gathering around for prayer and each time someone was sent to let us in.

Another problem was often the breakdown of the equipment, one time we had to change the projector three times. When we gathered around the third one, laid hands on it and prayed, binding Satan, it worked. Several times, there was a horrible scream, and the movie screen was torn in half by some unseen hand, so we prayed and replaced it.

The enemy is always present at these showings and tries to interfere because there are each time hundreds, often thousands, who give their lives to Jesus Christ. We know that there have been 6 billion total viewers, because of the little Salvation slips which w be filled out by the viewers, and they come afterwards to the lights for our supplies.

ANOTHER POWERFUL WAY TO REACH THEM

Having shared with you in one of my previous books about having been a part of the ministry of Global Media Outreach. Having been given the reports which say that over 741 e-mails were sent by me in two years and now it will increase. Always giving Colossians 1:13 as the first scripture, which says "He has delivered us from the power of darkness and transferred us into the kingdom of the of the Son of His love."

Making sure that my thanks were constant to the Lord, being so grateful for using me with those He brought into my life. He continues in verse :14 "In Whom we have redemption through His blood, the forgiveness of sins." They loved getting these verses which assured them that they now belonged to this great God for all eternity.

Being thankful also for letting my family and I live this blessed life, which our beloved Savior has made possible for us, so we can be fruitful in His harvest. As it tells us in Hebrews 13:15

"Therefore by Him let us continually offer the sacrifice of praise to God, that is the fruit of our lips, giving thanks to His name."

Depending on His participation in every part of my life, I do not have to live in fear of anything that lies ahead. I have read the end of the book. Knowing from all my past experiences with my God, that whatever trial comes up has gone past Him, and will be for my growth. I have seen that I do not have to face it in my own strength.

One thing I am sure of is written in Romans 1:16, "For I am not ashamed of the Gospel of Christ, for it is the power of God to salvation for everyone who believes." This is my courage and assurance when I am witnessing about this Creator, who has died for everyone in the world, believer or not.

THIS GOD NEVER STOPS HIS PROVISION

It is so true, as it says in Philippians 4:19 that our God has supplied all our needs according to His riches in glory by Christ Jesus. My children and I have never been in need of anything in the 48 years we have walked with this generous Lord. Therefore, the enemy has not been able to cause us to live in fear.

Even the precious years my boys and I were living in the mountains we learned our Lord's faithful provisions never stop. Whenever we shared with others what our Lord gave, it always came back to us. These seven years we lived up there, this trustworthy God gave such precious memories, and we still talk and laugh about them when we are together.

It was such an awesome revelation to me when my Savior said in John 7:37 "If anyone thirsts, let him come to me and drink," and then in verse :38 He continues "He who believes in Me, as the scripture has said, out of his heart will flow rivers of living water." This means to me that the water is His beloved Word, which, as I take it in, will then flow out of me.

This is such a treasure, and I am forever grateful to Him. I can just vision this happening as the Savior has allowed me to bring this miraculous, live saving message all over the world, and to the youth in this country. This is so awesome, to me, I have received the Holy Spirit, Who is from God, so I can know all that has been revealed so far.

Even those painful years during World War II in Germany, God's powerful protection could never be explained, had they not been controlled by Him. It only makes sense that He knew we would belong to Him someday. This is so awesome to me; I wonder if I will ever know all about this wonderful unimaginable Creator.

His miraculous care did not come to memory until I had become a Christian in California in July of 1974 through Campus Crusade for Christ. It became the most wonderful and blessed day of my life and Arrowhead Springs my most loved place in the US. Tears still come to my eyes every time I recall the awesome patience of this loving God.

RIDING MOTORCYCLES AGAIN

At the age of seventeen, I loved riding motorcycles with my friends up to the German-Swiss mountains with great joy. We would take these adventures until I moved as an exchange student for a year to Switzerland. It was at the end of that adventure that I returned home and met my future husband, who brought me to California.

After becoming a Christian through Campus Crusade, now called CRU one of my special adventures in-country, was to the wonderful gathering of the Christian Motorcyclists Association. Still enjoying the memories and pictures about their gathering in Philadelphia, at a large and famous park, with activities daily.

I have shared that my job with CRU has been "Donor Relations" this means relating the latest reports of God's work through us to all who gave. Each one of our team has what is called a caseload of donors to be contacted regularly, encouraged and prayed for. One of my donors was the "Christian Motorcyclists Association." I worked with them, and they gave generously to our world-wide ministries.

They had sent their large gift to the Jesus Film, and I was asked to pick up the check at their yearly rally in Philadelphia, at a famous park. Staying three days at their rally was an honor, and I truly enjoyed the Bible times and awesome worship. I got the chance to ride on several motorcycles each day, and my children and grandchildren loved to share the pictures with their friends.

LIVING BY THE LORD'S PLAN IS SO SAFE

Each of my mission trips were so unique because in each country I got to live with our national Campus Crusade staff. This was so special because on our days off we would go to places that were seldom seen and were save for me to go to. The ministries were a true blessing because so many became Christians and received Bibles in their own language.

This loving God says to His children in 1 Corinthians 2:12, "Now we have received, not the spirit of the world, but the Spirit Who is from God, that we might know the things that have been freely given to us by God." This has always been so awesome to me that without having earned it in any way, it was freely given to me.

This makes me try to do something to earn it, however no matter how hard I try, it is wrong, my God says it is a gift. The Bible says in Isaiah 64:6 that all my righteousness's are like filthy rags, so I better live in His peace and rest. It has truly been a joy to accept His commands and lovingly respond back with love, that is His only longing.

My prayers are that this merciful God will save America, since He governs the affairs of men, He is the only One who can do this. It says so beautifully in 1Timothy 2:1 and 2, "Therefore I exhort first of all, that supplications, prayers, intercessions, and giving of thanks be made for all men, for kings and all who are in authority."

This is what Moses did when God was going to destroy His people, he prayed, and God relented from destruction in Exodus 32:11 and :14 "So the Lord relented from the harm which He said He would do to His people. Another time was in Jonah 3:10 "Then God saw their works, that they turned from their evil way, and God relented from the disaster that He had planned to bring upon them, and He did not do it."

However, my favorite on these subjects is in Proverbs 21:1 where it says, "The king's (ruler's) heart is in the hand of the Lord, like the rivers of water, He turns it wherever He wishes." These scriptures make me truly live in the peace of God, seeing His wonderful fairness in all situations of life.

IT HAS BEEN SUCH A JOYFUL JOURNEY WITH MY SAVIOR

If anyone would have told me how life changing and adventurous my walk with my God would be, I might have pulled back in fear. However, doing it a step at a time and in His perfect plan, it was easy. First of all, it went by His knowledge of me, giving me only what He knew this child of His could handle, and make her eventually what He had planned for her to be.

The awesome times of coming to know Him and His indescribable faithfulness, I could never write it all down. Each of His chosen would learn in their own way, I have seen that my God does not like uniformity, He loves variety. Having experienced Him working around my own will, He brought gently His own perfect will to happen.

The staff families I got to live with in those 27 countries, as we came to love each other, we wrote out pretend adoption papers. We knew we would get to live together for all eternity, so this was just an early commitment. Worshipping our awesome Creator together became our daily privilege and joy.

Each of my many trips to Jerusalem included Bethlehem and Nazareth, where we had friends and co-workers. It was so interesting as we got to stop at places we knew from the Bible. Like on the way to Nazareth, we stopped at the hill where they wanted to throw Jesus off, and other places we were familiar with from Jesus' life on earth.

It was like when I stood with my feet in the Sea of Galilee, watching many believers getting baptized, bringing back some blessed memories from the Bible. Knowing we get to see it all when the new Jerusalem has come to earth, is worthwhile waiting for. When I imagine experiencing it with the people I love, makes time pass much to slow.

With all I have learned about my amazing God and His perfect plan, my own imagination goes soring and makes me so grateful I am His. Having experienced much of His world, and yet only a part of it, makes it hard to wait for more. I never could have dreamed of what life and the future with my Creator God would be like.

KNOWING WHERE TO GO FOR HELP

Whenever I got too critical of someone, I ran to my Savior and asked for His intervention. Criticism always made things harder and caused others to respond back in the same way, which never solved anything. It took me a while before I learned to accept things as they are before I became less selfish.

Jesus said so beautifully in John 14:27 "Peace I leave with you, My peace I give to you, not as the world gives do I give to you. Let not your heart be troubled, neither let it be afraid." This advice is so meaningful as I am now seeking peace and am trying to accept things as they are rather than wanting to change them.

The enemy loves to bring up situations which will remove that wonderful peace but admitting that my ways are not always the right ones, will begin the healing. The Grace that is so freely given for my Salvation, as it says in Ephesians 2:8, for by Grace you have been saved and it is a gift from God.

My beloved God has such powerful and comforting promises in the love letter to His children, which should never allow fear. One of those that bring hope and comfort to my life is Romans

4:7 and 8 which claims that "Blessed are those whose lawless deeds are forgiven and whose sins are covered."

Blessed I am indeed, having learned to put my trust in my awesome God who promises in Hebrews 13:8 that He is the same yesterday, today and forever. This means I don't ever have to be afraid that He changes His feelings about me. It causes me to live in that perfect rest He promises His children.

So, with that assurance, am I going to sit with my Savior by a beautiful lake, leave my concerns in His capable hands and enjoy Him! He left His beautiful heaven and died the most terrible death so I can live the abundant life with Him forever. Would it not offend Him if I spend my life in fear and worry? No, I will love Him, serve Him and share His deep love with those who don't know Him.

BLESSINGS TRULY COME FROM TIME IN GOD'S WORD

It is so important to my God for me to come to know Him, most of my favorite verses are on that subject. One of the ways is written in Isaiah 30:21 saying, "Your ears shall hear a word behind you, saying, this is the way, walk in it." This can only develop if I spend much of my time in His faithful instructions.

In the mission trip to Botswana, one of the countries in Africa, we started our days of witnessing in prayer and some encouraging songs from our churches. These songs told us not to fear, which we needed before we brought the Gospel of our God to the businesspeople in the city. It always worked for us.

We started out each having bags full of our Jesus Films which we gave the managers of the stores and our witnessing booklets to the employees. The success was unbelievable, and we invited all to the Film showings at night. Our spirits were high each day as we returned to our room and counted those blessed response slips .

It would have been impossible for me to have imagined being a part of something so blessed and wonderful. My beloved Lord drew me into His amazing kingdom work, never to let me leave it. Only He knows my grateful heart and eternal commitment to our future together. My greatest desire is to lead so many more into His waiting arms.

It was such a blessing to sit together evenings and sing our favorite worship songs and share the stories of our witnessing times during the day. We always made sure that we gave our God all the glory and we laughed at some mistakes we made. Our time always went by way to fast, and we looked forward to sharing our adventures when we got back home.

AM I LETTING SATAN DISCOURAGE ME?

Where am I spending my time, what is mostly on my mind, what am I giving my attention to? These questions caused me to check what useless stuff I have in my home or in my plans. Well, I was shocked and began cleaning out some things but then I had to decide what to do with all the stuff I wanted to keep. I was just amazed how much was not needed.

Gratefully I realized that there wasn't too much extra on my mind anymore. After walking and ministering with my beloved God for forty-eight years much of the useless stuff has finally gone to the background. The Lord has brought some new brothers and sisters into my life with whom I want to spend some positive time.

I got so much peace and encouragement for my life from Hebrews 4:12 which says "For the Word of God is living and powerful and sharper than any two-edged sword" which made me want to have an even more solid foundation. I longed to have a clearer way to tell others why I believe what I believe.

It was easy for me to start a conversation and lead into the spiritual subject if there was time. However, I wanted to be able to get more direct to the Salvation approach when there was an opportunity. My joy of leading others to my beloved Savior is still there and I long to be used for His purpose whenever needed.

It continues in verse :12 that this sword " pierces even to the division of soul and spirit and joints and marrow". Wow, it could not possibly go any deeper, leaving nothing which is not totally exposed to this powerful and loving God. So, I had stopped a long time ago pretending with my Lord since He knows all about me already.

This awesome Creator finishes this Hebrew verse :12 telling me that He "is a discerner of the thoughts and intents of my heart." This leaves absolutely nothing I can hide from Him, and it finally helped me to be totally honest and open with my Lord. This began a very close and personal relationship which lasted till today and I pray lasts forever.

REFUSING TO BE CONFORMED TO THIS WORLD.

In the beginning of my Christian life, when my Savior explained to me about not being conformed to this world in Romans 12:1, I knew what He meant. This had been my way of life before He entered it. But then He went on in verse :2 that I need now to be forever transformed by the renewing of my mind, and I prayed for this.

It was not easy because this is where Satan had guided me in my past lost and lonely years. However now I was much of my time in the precious, saving Word of my God and each day something changed. That blessed verse ;12 ends saying that I may prove what is that good and acceptable and perfect will of God.

By my Savior's grace He has helped to fulfill that awesome command and it is my blessing and joy to finish that way. By continuing in His will instead of mine, helps me to draw strength in everything that comes into my life. Letting Jesus be in control of all I do and say "here I am Lord, use me," has been my prayer and He brought it about.

There is no stopping what He has called me for, this must be why I am still here at 85, my Lord will finish what He has started. Since He has a plan for me, who am I to question it or change it? While still in this world, I will be as available to be used by my Savior as ever.

Nothing and no one can separate me from His love, as He tells me so strong and beautiful in Romans 8:38 & 39 which says, “”For I am persuaded that neither death nor life, nor angels nor demons, nor powers, nor things present nor things to come, nor height nor depth, nor any other created thing, shall be able to separate us from the love of God, which is in Christ Jesus our Lord.”

FOCUSING ON HIS PROMISES AND ADVICE

It is my firm decision not to let the enemy control my emotions or discourage me. As so far, my instructions will, as always in the past, come from my Father's truthful Word. Satan will always try to convince me that all I have done was useless, but this is one of his favorite lies. My success is in my Creator, and He never leaves me

Who is this enemy who is jealous over my future? I am able to tell him that his future is in a very dark and hot place, separated from this glorious God of love. This same God tells me my work has been what He has chosen me for, and it will continue while still on this earth.

Having learned not to focus on what is missing in my life and what might be impossible for me to achieve, made me dwell on all my God has given me. It has been more than I could have ever imagined, and my gratefulness is without end. It has been so awesome to experience that all my troubles were in the hands of my powerful Father.

Concentrating on the Lord's proclaimed will for his children, made me keep my eyes on the love-letter written to them. One of the items needing to be changed was my speech. Going by the advice of 1Peter 3:10, was "For he who would love life and see good days, let him refrain his tongue from evil, and his lips from speaking deceit."

It was one of the earliest lessons my Savior taught me because it had to be cleaned up before I could do any teaching. Becoming familiar with His likes and dislikes, my tongue had to be worthy to proclaim His Word. Knowing my solution would come, made me truly listen for His corrections from His precious voice.

Not only did my battles belong to the Lord but all those changes did as well. Needing to always know what mine and my children's future held, it was such a relieve when He taught me to live one day at a time. There was unbelievable freedom and peace in this, and it relieved also any stress.

Another relieve came from limiting fear, as He kept assuring me of His unconditional love and never ending forgiveness. As Jesus said in His prayer example, in Luke 11:2, forgive us our sins for we forgive those indebted to us. Forgiveness brings great peace and relieve to bad memories that have taken my joy in the past.

ALL GOD HAS PROMISED HE WILL DO

In the 48 years of walking with my God I have been most of all impressed by His great faithfulness. Being obedient to what He says brings blessings even if it is scary or uncomfortable at the time. It says in His Word in Psalms 33:14 and 15, "From the place of His dwelling He looks on all the inhabitants of the earth."

But listen how this Savior continues in verse :15, "He fashions their hearts individually, He considers all their works." Wow, He fashions my heart individually, I love this because He is not talking to a church or some Christian group, but to each of us. This makes His love so personal and intimate, and I want to respond by loving Him back.

Why would I want to wait, when He is willing to walk me through my next lesson which it is for my growth. I need to hear who He is: the light, the way, the living bread, the open door and the living water and the truth. He took the time to see a lady who was getting water and told in John 4:10 that He would have given her living water if she asked.

Besides, the Lord told me in Matthew 25:40 "Assuredly, I say to you, inasmuch as you did it to one of the least of these My brethren, you did it to Me." This makes me strongly want to do something with all He has given me. This God has put in me a desire to pray for others and to commune with Him.

If praying is not real to me, I am afraid that my Savior is not real to me. The two are totally connected and are of no use to me without each other. So, I will keep praying and even increase it, since praying makes my beloved Lord closer in my life. By praying daily for those I know and care about, gives me a chance to bring them before Him and be a small part of their Christian life.

BEING FAITHFUL WITH WHAT GOD HAS GIVEN

Once again, this favorite verse in Isaiah 55:10, here it is " For as the rain comes down, and the snow from heaven, and do not return there, but water the earth, :11 so shall My word be that goes forth from My mouth, it shall not return to Me void, but it shall accomplish what I please, and it shall prosper in the thing for which I sent it."

This is dear to my heart because I keep reminding my Father that His precious word is sent for Salvation and that is for those in my prayers. Daily I reminded Him of it as I raised my children, especially when they started a life of their own. When they were no longer under my care, they needed to be even more under His guidance and teaching.

Why would my Lord show me the next step if I have not been faithful in what He already provided? It was something to pay close attention to because the enemy loves getting me side tract. The parable Jesus gave about His Word being the seeds and the varieties of grounds it fell on is a great example.

Since my Creator had given me access to the lives of my children, grand and great-grandchildren, I took my teaching them very seriously. These seeds of the knowledge of God were precious and were for a lifetime, so making them fall in fertile ground was important. I was so relieved learning that my responsibility was only that they heard, then the Holy Spirit would take over.

That was such a weight of my shoulders, and my reaction was an increase of prayer for them. This is also why I love Luke 10:19 where Jesus promises that "He gives us authority over all the power of the enemy." This meant so much when opposing Satan on their behalf once they started school. Jesus said, "and nothing shall by any means hurt us."

Wow, that powerful promise really minimized my fear of the enemy and made my prayers bolder than ever. The girls seemed to have more trouble than the boys and I saw their God's loving intervention. Those of them who took my advice about daily time in their Bibles even raised their grades to the top.

CHOOSE MY WORDS TO HEAL-NOT HURT

My gratefulness to my Creator was shown by even more thinking of and talking with this saving God and abiding to His instructions. Living more in the joy of His word, gave me the strength to face whatever Satan tried to throw my way. Confronting what takes my peace from me, makes me hand it over to my Savior who will solve it.

Being aware of how my Lord tells me to help in using what He has already given me makes a big difference. Having worked with so many high schoolers made me sensitive to most of their likes and dislikes. No matter how much it was my desire to help, it was not easy because their home situations were only known to me by their word.

After the last three years of having become an active part of The Joy Company, a Ministry to city schools, the Lord gave me a new idea. A meeting with over thirty high-school youths for leadership training, was from 5:30 to 8:30. These young people were amazing in wanting to be teachers to other students, doing it with the knowledge of God.

I started also as a mentor for the four oldest girls in the group which I specially befriended. The Joy Co trains the youth with a wonderful Leadership Program and Bible studies. These youths long to be leaders in their schools and future job positions and we are proud of them as are their parents. We had just graduated another twenty, who gave their testimonies of what they had learned.

My four girls were chosen because their Savior put them on my mind. The pastor and parents had to agree to this, and I will stay in touch with them when possible. However, for all activities I get wisdom first of all from our God, without that nothing takes place. Sharing my past experiences and the love of God will give them some special start in life.

BE ALWAYS READY TO PASS IT ON

In this way, what my God has taught me all these years has another way of benefitting those who seek Him. If they are willing to give Him control of their lives, they will find peace and joy as well as guidance. I will share with them that there is no shame if their knowledge is not great yet, only in pretending to have it.

To be real to family and friends is important to me because I want them to come to me in search for the word of God. He said to come and ask, and He will give it to all liberally and without reproach in James 1:5 and it will be given. This awesome promise will benefit them greatly and they can pass it on also.

Another of my mission trips took me to the country Botswana, a part of Africa, and it was a true joy because of the large number of converts. After leaving Johannesburg, it was a short flight to our planned mission work. Botswana is very interesting as well as beautiful, our lodging was covered with Africa's most beautiful bright colored flowers and trees.

Because the temperature was seventy all the time, we were able to eat our meals on the lovely patio. In the mornings we met early, after breakfast, for half an hour of worship and prayer and our favorite songs. In high spirits we each loaded up some bags of Jesus Films and witnessing booklets and climbed in our van.

Starting at the big grocery stores, we went, always in teams of two and visited the smaller shops. Around noon we spread out at the very large outdoor markets and spoke with the owners. In no time we were surrounded by the customers, and all wanted to listen to "The Four Spiritual Laws."

BEING INSPIRED MEANS "IT JUICES US UP"

It was such a blessing and those who did not speak English had the others interpret for them. We were amazed by their desire to hear God's message and we invited them to the evenings Jesus Film showings. Every showing was at a different parking lot so they would be close enough to come.

At the changing of the film reel, one of us would share their testimony and they usually picked me to speak. After the showing those who said the Salvation prayer were asked to come to the lights and receive a Gospel of Luke. Of course, both the film, and the materials were always in their own language, and they loved it.

This is what I feel when writing, because the ideas or memories come flowing while putting them down and I get to relive it all. Like this morning someone was talking about the wedding in Cana and the writer was John. How would he have known what Mary said to Jesus and what the man said in verse :10 about the wine being the best.

It tells in verse :6 that there were six water pots holding thirty gallons of top-quality wine each. I love that story because Jesus totally bypassed the four-year fermentation process as well as the growing, harvesting, smashing and sifting. No one else but God could have pulled that of. Of course, top vines take much longer than that, as vintners will brag about. Most miracles involved illnesses so this one must have been fun for our Savior.

After my prayer of Salvation, there was such an assurance of what I read in the Bible every day was true. I could not get enough of what this Savior said was mine to believe and claim. This whole transformation came from my gracious Lord, and I enjoyed yielding to it. Now I wanted more than anything for my family to find this peaceful and content existence.

My two boys, being four and six then, learned about God's existence from me. However, my girls, being fourteen and sixteen, and I, heard it from our church and the lady who led me to the Lord. Later my ex-husband Bill prayed to be saved with my son Steve, who was leaving for his term in the Army. This was also two months before his father's death.

However, the rest of my family wanted no part of this Salvation and told me not to bring my God in their homes. My heart was sad; however this did not keep me from continuing to grow and come to know this God better. Finally, after eight years of praying and trusting God with them, all entered the kingdom that year.

I began to be more juiced up at this time and it was then that my God gave me a job at the evangelical ministry of Campus Crusade for Christ. Having become a Christian through this God ordained mission, work was a blessing and a continuous learning. My Creator also began to give me the personal ministries I have told you about.

Having seen that my God's promises are for real and trustworthy, I put my mind at ease and let Him show me my purpose for being here. His transforming me was only by His influence and not by my being more holy. It was not anything that could be accomplished by my efforts. Everything came by reading His word and listening for His precious voice.

Realizing that only He can give me that abundant life He promised in John 10:10 and He continues about being the good Shepherd. Having taught on this so many times, especially to my young, incarcerated students, was a great joy. They loved it, as did I, that His sheep, in verse :27 hear His voice, He knows them, and they follow Him.

They loved this so much because almost all of them had just received that awesome Salvation. As I shared before, they had very recently written their names in my book and after saying that special prayer had given Him their life. After being saved, they got to draw a small cross by their name which was very special to them.

This scripture continues with a very powerful promise in verse :28, where He says, " I give them eternal life, and they shall never perish." After explaining to them what perish means and that they will never go to that place, some of them cried as I had done. Revealing to them that this is why their Savior died for them, their gratefulness was real.

My favorite thing, for thirty-five years, was convincing these precious youths that their Savior's promises never change, because He never changes. Most of them were in Juvenile Hall for three month some longer than this and a few for one year. Even though the Lord had given me other ministries, this one was so important to me because these youths would be back out where no Bible was taught, unless it was in their heart.

WE ARE ABRAHAM'S SEED

Only my Savior can give that abundant life and joy in all I do and experience His wonderful peace. This comes by spending precious time with Him in His Word. Where else could these gifts and blessings be found. Harping on this the most is because that is how I found it these forty-eight years, and it is the only place I can continue to seek it out.

My Lord tells me in Hebrews 2:16 "For indeed, He does not give aid to angels, but He does give aid to the seed of Abraham." So, I wanted to make sure that is my position and I looked it up. So, He explains in Galatians3:7 that only those who are of faith are sons of Abraham. Well this is good but there is more, Galatians 3:29 assures me "and if you are Christ's, then you are Abraham's seed, and heirs according to the promise"

Wow, that kept me informed for sure, and I am very happy that He indeed gives me aid. This is exactly what my Father has done all these years I have lived in His presence. My gratefulness comes in so many ways because His aid has come in such a variety of ways. Once my children were raised a whole new way of aid was needed.

The Holy Spirit was required by me in a powerful way as I was now working with and teaching other people's children. So, seeking this beloved Helper was almost constantly, even more than with my own kids. And here He was, faithfully guiding me but also protecting me from parents who might object to my instructing their child from the Bible.

Needing this God desperately for myself, I was greatly comforted by Jesus' promise in John 14:26 "But the Helper the Holy Spirit Whom the Father will send in my name, He will teach you all things and bring to your remembrance all things that I said to you." This greatly encouraged me to continue with what He had called me for.

CONTINUE SERVING WITH A WHOLE HEART

Cooperating with the Holy Spirit meant being in touch with Him the best I could. In times of failure or busyness with other things, confession closed the gap again because He never moved. When other people's voices came into my mind, I would deal with them but not let them settle in.

Our instructions are in 1John 4 :6 "We are of God. He who knows God hears us, he who is not of God does not hear us. By this we know the Spirit of truth and the spirit of error. And it continues in verse :7 " Beloved let us love one another, for love is of God, and everyone who loves is born of God and knows God."

This beloved Creator has put me in situations where I needed Him and had to seek His presence. One of them was that my sons had to grow up without a father in their lives. The younger one dealt with it easier, however the older one suffered over it. Being so grateful that our church had a few men who were sensitive of this and would now and then take one or the other to ball games and beach trips with their own kids.

Being aware of single moms in our church I would pick them up for our church programs, movies and sport games. Even in later years there were incidences where one of them would come up someplace and recall my help which blessed us both. I have learned that whatever good I did for others came back to me and brought gratefulness.

These days were such a blessing, as our gracious God kept helping and leading us to go the right way. It was always a great joy when my sons and I had a chance to tell anyone about this merciful and loving God. We never got tired of this, and our Lord kept blessing us by giving us more chances to share His Salvation plan.

GOD'S PLAN FOR THIS BLESSED SALVATION

One of my favorite subjects to teach on is Ephesians 1:4, "Blessed be the God and Father of our Lord Jesus Christ, Who has blessed us with every spiritual blessing in the heavenly places in Christ. Just as He chose us in Him before the foundation of the world, that we should be holy and without blame before Him in love."

Wow, I can remember my amazement when this came up in my Bible study, reading it again and again. To imagine how long ago He knew me and how He kept me alive all this time. Remembering and now sharing, since I became His, the many things He has done in my life and used me for. I could never be anything but grateful and share my Creator's love and mercy.

I have written before, about the wartime in Germany, when our God saved my mom, my two sisters and I from being killed. There were many times but three specific ones, when His protection was very noticeable, because He knew we would be His someday. Not imagining I would ever come to the USA, my Savior had already worked it all out long ago.

With the beautiful promise Jesus gave, that because I live, you shall live also, in John 14:19, helped me to keep my eyes on Him. This opened the door to dwell in that peace He provided. My Lord has given all that I need, plus the strength, to do what He asks of me. Even when I mess up, He gives me hope by showing me that when I have blown it, He does not forsake me.

In 1 Corinthians 10:13 it says that no temptation has overtaken me, but such as is common to man. This God is faithful, Who will not allow me to be tempted beyond what I am able, but with the temptation will also make a way of escape. This way I may be able to bear it. That is so awesome, even though I would never take advantage of it.

LET MY SAVIOR HAVE HIS WAY

My Savior is bigger than anything I can come up with or anything Satan could persuade me to do. My God has taught me early not give Him limits, but to enjoy His greatness. There is no one He can be compared with because He is a Creator as well as Savior, so how could I possibly trust someone more than Him.

My life with Him has been joyful and content and I never regretted following this indescribable God, not even for a moment. He has transformed me by renewing my mind, so, I have tried to prove what is that good and perfect will of God. As long as my time was spent in His precious love letter, obeying His commends was possible.

I can do all things through Christ my Savior; He gives me the conviction to do well and promises in Psalms 32:8 that He will guide me with His eyes. Jesus was going to Samaria to save a woman with a bad reputation. He did not look at what her live was like, even though He knew it. He even revealed Himself as the Messiah to her and she persuaded her village to come and meet Him, saying 'could this be the Christ?'

Moses made mistakes too and yet God used Him greatly, even at 120 years old he was capable and had his full eyesight. I am going to be 85 on November 11th yet do not want to hit 90, having waited so long to be with my beloved God. But, as long as He uses me to lead other to Him, I will stick around a little longer, not that there is a choice.

There is nothing more precious than walking with a God who loves me and thinks I am worth to be used in His wonderful work. He even spoke through a donkey to get His work done, which shows His great sense of humor. And He showed His sense of humor when He chose someone like me to work in His perfect plan.

A HEALED PAST AND A JOYFUL FUTURE

Having shared my painful_past in my first book, and my wartime in my third book, I can now write about the learning and growing. Having learned to refuse every suggestion and thought coming from the enemy, allows me to have my mind more on God's word. This makes my life so much more joyful and filled with the peace of my Creator.

This way my future will continue in what He has called me for. As I write, the Holy Spirit feeds me subjects and reminds me of useful scriptures to share with you. Even my house is now a home of praise and prayer. Grace is looking for anyone to save and heal because that Grace is the person of Jesus Christ.

Some happenings can only be explained by God working His awesome plan. These miracles make no natural sense because they are supernatural. They happen in every day and in every part of the world and I am one of the CRU staff who gets these reports. Sharing them with my faithful supporters and the donors of this great ministry keeps me joyful.

There are some valuable warnings in the Creators powerful book to make His children aware of danger. One of them is in 2 Corinthians 11:14 and 15 tells me that Satan **transforms himself into an angel of light and so can his helpers.** That is why it is so important that we know the truth from His Word and stay familiar with it.

My sister was a manager in her bank and told us that their new employees only handle and count and stack the real money. This way, when the bank throws in a counterfeit bill, the employees recognize it instantly. That is why it is so important that God's children know the truth from His Word, to identify Satan's lies and deceptions.

THERE IS ONLY ONE GOD

This awesome Creator identifies Himself many times and one of my favorites is in Isaiah 43: 11 starts with "I, even I, am the Lord, and besides Me there is no savior." He cannot be clearer than that, besides revealing and explaining Himself throughout His powerful book which covers every subject in life.

It also explains Jesus as a captain when Joshua sees Him in Joshua 5:13—15 it tells us " And it came to pass, when he lifted his eyes and behold a Man stood opposite him with his sword drawn in His hand. And Joshua went to Him and said, "Are you for us or for our adversaries?"

It continues in verse :14 So He said "No, but as Commander of the army of the Lord I have now come." Joshua asked, "what does my Lord say to His servant?" :15 Then the Commander said to Joshua, "Take your sandals off your feet, for the place where you stand is holy" And Joshua did so. I just love Jesus being portrayed in that way, because He will never again be Who He was in His earthly body.

It also says so beautifully in Zechariah 3:3 "Now Joshua, was clothed with filthy garments and was standing before the Angel.

In verse :4 He said to those standing before Him "Take away the filthy garments from him," and to him He said, "See, I have removed your iniquity from you, and I will clothe you with rich robes."

I enjoy that so much because I imagine that Jesus said the same thing to me after I received Him as my Lord and Savior. I did not have to walk in shame since then, because He welcomed me, never to be separated from Him again. This same Angel of the Lord has saved and cleaned up everyone who came to God through Jesus.

BEING ONE IN THE SPIRIT

When Jesus left the earth to return to the Father, He promised to prepare a place for us and then come back to get us. But then He explained in John 16: 7 "Nevertheless, I tell you the truth. It is to your advantage that I go away, for if I do not go away, the Helper will not come to you, but if I depart, I will send Him to you."

Then Jesus continues, in verse :13, "However, when He, the Spirit of truth has come, He will guide you into all truth." Having been able to experience this Spirit, especially in all my overseas trips, I could truly count on Him. All those times at the bus changes and the train and airplane transfers, He gave calmness and patience.

Also in those daily training sessions and conferences overseas, His peace was with the teachers wanting to learn the Bible. These precious people enjoyed getting familiar with the life of Jesus and His awesome promises. Feeling the presence of the Holy Spirit gave us great encouragement to make it sound real and true.

Also, in my 35 years teaching the Bible in The Juvenile Detention Center, there were so many times I had to depend on the Holy Spirit. Even though I had my lessons prepared, my mind was sometimes side tract, and He graciously called me back. Especially when someone's question was on a different subject, this precious Spirit recalled the right answer for me.

With the thousands of youths at Camp Pendleton Marine base the three hours a night three days a week would not have been possible. This Holy Spirit held up my energy and awareness because often I got tired before these young Bible students did. The same was my need of depending on Him on the days when volunteering at The Pregnancy Center saving babies and moms.

Once a month, these moms could come and pick up the needs for their little ones. Most of these mothers we helped were single and were provided for by the Government. However, when counseling or praying with them I needed the Spirit's wisdom. It was important not to offend in anyway because the Center had to keep a good reputation. I could not possibly tell even a part of what this wonderful Teacher and Guide has done for me.

KEEP ABIDING IN THE VINE

My teachings are often on John 15:1 and 2, where my Savior says, "I am the true Vine, and My Father is the vinedresser." For some reason I can relate to being one of those branches and drawing from that precious sap flowing from Him. It is such a powerful instruction when He says in verse :4 "abide in Me, and I in you,"

"As the branch cannot bear fruit of itself, unless it abides in the vine, neither can you, unless you abide in Me." Abiding in my Savior was the most powerful thing I had to obey in order to make it through these 48 years I have known Him. It is so true what He says at the end, "without Me you can do nothing."

That is why I am so grateful when Jesus says in Matthew 19:26 "With men this is impossible, but with God all things are possible." My two daughters were 15 and 17 when I became a Christian, each of them ten years older than their brothers. Both of my girl's boyfriends also received Christ as their Savior and the four of them got baptized and then married.

These boyfriends became their husband's, however they had many trials in their marriages because being a Christian was something new to them. That is the difference with my son's, they were five and seven when I gave my life to the Savior. Having joined a Bible teaching church, between the church and me, they were raised in the knowledge of God.

Because the rest of my family did not want to hear the beautiful message of the Gospel, I could spend all my time teaching my boys. We began the wonderful habit of spending the first time of the day, in different corners of the living room reading the Word. This was not always perfect, because these young ones, as I, had our thoughts go astray but this improved with time.

However eventually the scriptures took root in their hearts, and they began to share what they learned. Beginning to be blessed by their growth, I told them that our Lord wanted more than that morning time. So, what He showed me was not to turn on the TV in the evening, until we first have half an hour in the Bible.

THIS FAITHFUL GOD NEVER FAILS US

I can truly vouch for His word coming true, and I took Proverbs 22:6 very seriously when it says "Train up a child in the way he should go, and when he is old he will not depart from it." This is why, these boys hearing the truth was so very important to me, and the Lord showed me another way for them to hear that truth.

Our Church had a youth program called AWANA, where they received a patch for their uniforms. These patches were given by memorizing scriptures according to the subject of their book, which had the number of verses given. My boys loved it because after so many books finished, they received a trophy. As a leader for the girls, I was allowed to join them in this program.

I have already shared that I became a leader for high school girls and some of the blessings from that. My point it to tell how important it is to memorize scriptures, because when the enemy comes to deceive, they will not always have a Bible handy. I learned how vital it is to have a scripture ready to quote as Jesus did in Matthew 4:3-11 "it is written."

When Satan tempted Him in the desert and the Savior answered with scriptures, Satan had to leave. It is so clear in James

4:7 where it says "Therefore submit to God. Resist the devil and he will flee from you." I get so exited when the Holy Spirit gives me Bible wisdom to match up with what I want to share.

Until the Lord wrote these five books, I never realized how perfect His wisdom matches our daily needs. So, any scripture will suffice in getting rid of the enemy. So, use the most popular one John 3:16 "For God so loved the world that He gave His only begotten Son, that whoever believes in Him should not perish but have everlasting life." This scripture has gotten me through many troubles.

IF MY PEOPLE, WHO ARE CALLED BY MY NAME

Having used this scripture before, this is one where our powerful God promises to heal our land. He promises in 2Chronicles 7:14 "If My people who are called by My name will humble themselves, and pray and seek My face, and turn from their wicked ways, then I will hear from heaven, and will forgive their sin and heal their land."

Most of God's promises are unconditional, but this is one that has conditions. Having promised to keep what He has requested, I feel I need to be more regular in my performance of them. Always having longed to be more like my Savior, I still have a few things that should not be that important to me.

Trying not to ignore or close a door my loving God opened, I also tried never to open a door that He had already closed. More important has been never to go through a door that Satan opens. The only way I have been able to do this is by being in my Savior's word as often as I can.

That is the only way I can know the difference, this is the only way I learn to recognize if I am hearing my Fathers voice or the enemy's. I harp on and teach on being in God's word more than anything else, because I have seen absolute miracles through this. Especially through the change in the lives of my grand and great-grandchildren.

Their attitudes and school-grades were so bad, and the only way those were changed was by them listening to the above advice in the Bible-studies I gave them . One of them even raised her grades to all A's which encouraged others to follow. Starting with just fifteen minutes a day she raised it soon to more and ended high school with four different awards, and a good job at the YWCA.

THE WAY THE TRUTH AND THE LIFE

Jesus the Savior explained His relations with the Father so beautiful in John 14:1,2 where He says, " Let not your heart be troubled, you believe in God, believe also in Me. In My Father's house are many mansions, if it were not so, I would have told you. I go to prepare a place for you."

He continues in verse :3, "And if I go and prepare a place for you, I will come again and receive you to Myself, that where I am, there you may be also." This is such an awesome promise, my heart not only rejoiced but was so comforted about my future. There was such peace in me to know for sure that my children and those I love and pray for will be with our Savior forever.

God's promises do not always come true instantly, but they always come true. Once in a while, He already answered before I even spoke the prayer out and I gratefully accepted and thanked Him. This was especially when my best friend had moved to another State, and I missed her. I longed for a new friend but had not asked the Lord yet.

I had attended a Messianic church and was seated next to a lady who introduced herself to me. I noticed a strong accent and asked her if she was from Germany to which she answered happily, yes, I am. We right away connected and enjoyed each other, especially when we realized we loved our God in a very deep way and could worship Him also in the German language.

This made me love my God even more because of His faithfulness to His children, and He showed that in so many ways. I began worshipping Him often and started memorizing Scriptures to share His word more confidently. One I memorized first was John 14:6 where my Savior says "I am the way, the truth and the life, no one comes to the Father but through Me." When I learned the Spanish language because I took two yearly mission trips to Mexico, I memorize that Scripture first.

HOW TO KNOW GOD'S WILL

Do I really involve my loving God in every part of my life, or only when I need Him. The only way I have learned is to read some scriptures and then get very still. Trying to hear and then write down what my God is saying truly helps. Sometimes it is clearer than others, I suppose it depends how important the subject is and am I really listening.

However, as I mentioned before, reading some scriptures and writing down what the impressions are, and what is my part in it, I found to be the best. He has never let me down, and if I missed an appointment with Him for whatever reason, there was a chance to make it up. It is amazing how faithful and generous this mighty God is.

In the beginning of my Christian life, there was jealousy in my heart for the believers who had always been walking with this awesome God. Most of their children were somewhere in ministry and had a good walk with God. It made me sad that my children and I wasted so much time till we lived a Christian life.

However, finally acknowledging and accepting my Lords love for us, I was able to thank Him with a whole heart. With my faith growing, I had to admit that my faithful God knew exactly the time my family and I would surrender our lives to Him. Then Satan had to find someone else to load his guilt trips on.

One of our many miracles was the way our Lord provided this last home, in which I am now living almost 18 years. I have already shared the lovely way He had moved us from a senior park to a family park. It was just in time for me to become a Guardian and take in one of my great grandchildren who was taken from her parents.

Being in a family park now, I was able to raise my sweet girl for six years and under the Lord's guidance, got to help her become a Jesus loving Christian. Now at eighteen, she is a high school graduate, with four awards and honor certificates and was called "Gymness of the year." By God's grace and guidance, she has grown into someone our family is proud of.

PRAYER CAN SAVE AMERICA

God governs the affairs of men, however, His promise to heal our land comes with a condition. He says very clearly in one of my favorite scriptures, 2 Chronicles 7:14, "if My people which are called by My name, shall humble themselves and pray, and seek My face, and turn from their wicked ways, then will I hear from heaven, and will forgive their sin, **and heal their land.** Wow, what a merciful promise which should surely be obeyed for our country's good.

God had planned to kill His people after they build and worshiped that golden calf, in Exodus 32:10 – God said "Now therefore, let Me alone, that My wrath may burn hot against them and that I may consume them. And I will make of you (Moses) a great nation. It continues in verse :11 "then Moses pleaded with the Lord his God and verse :14 tells us, "So the Lord relented from the harm which He said He would do to His people."

Wow, this is so comforting to know, that prayer can cause God to change His mind. Feeling strongly, that God would relent from allowing harm for America if enough of His children would pray for their beloved country. There is nothing this powerful, loving

God would deny His creation to give them a chance for a peaceful life on earth.

There was a similar incident with Nineveh, they repented when Jonah finally went and preached God's message. The Bible tells us in Jonah 3:10, "Then God saw their works, that they turned from their evil way, and God relented from the disaster that He had said He would bring upon them, and He did not do it," This gives me such hope for our country, if only the believers would pray and ask our merciful God to do this again.

NO SAFER PLACE THAN HIDDEN WITH CHRIST IN GOD

It was the same way in my life, when I finally surrendered it to this awesome Savior, I received a chance to start over. There was a new beginning for my four children and me, we began to live the way He had planned for us a long time ago. Like it tells us in Colossians 3:1-2, "If then you were raised with Christ, seek those things which are above, where Christ is, sitting at the right hand of God."

However, this is not all, because He continues in Colossians 3:3, "For you died and your life is hidden with Christ in God." There is no way the enemy could get close to me, unless I allow it. Satan could in no way make me do what he wants to, because my almighty God will give me the strength to withstand him. This is what I pray for all my Fathers children.

So often the Bible talks about seeds, especially in Jesus' parables. There are seeds hidden in so many things, like for instant apples, I just planted an apple tree in my yard. Now in my plum trees or my apricot tree, I know each seed could grow one tree. However, in my apple tree I could never know how many seeds are in one apple or how many of them would grow into trees. So it is, with the thousands of seeds God used me to sow in those He brings .

In the same way there is a certain pine tree in which cones the seeds are locked into. For instance, the Jack Pine, these cones will not release the seeds except in a hot fire. There was a time in my life when I had to go through such a fire, and my beloved Savior released some seeds He had planted in me. Through the fire He caused an amazing growth in my life and used those seeds to affect others after me.

I have to believe His word, and seek the knowledge from it, and protect what I am being taught. This way the enemy cannot take it from me. I have shared my favorite daily saying with you "What I focus on grows in me, and what grows in me I become." What I focus on first thing when I awaken, is greeting my beloved God, thanking Him for another safe and restful night and for another day closer to coming home.

JUST FALL IN LOVE WITH JESUS CHRIST

Having fallen in love with this awesome, loving Savior, I have been able to live with joy and peace in strange situations. I get to thank Him and love Him for all eternity, rejoicing with all those He has used me for. This merciful God had invited me to put on His yoke and then kept removing things my enemy threw my way.

The great thing is that it is not over until He says so, and when I joined Him, I became one spirit with Him. Jesus taught me to submit myself to His perfect plan, and to learn how to be that salt and light in Matthew 5:13, where He tells us, that we are the salt of the earth. However, if the salt loses its flavor, then it is good for nothing. It is the same with the light, what good is it if it is hidden under a basket?

That always fascinated me as I tried to figure out what salt does and wanted to teach His Word flavorfully and alive. The only way the word would not lose its taste, is by being read often, and thought about, not forgotten. So, I made sure that there were some lively examples for my students to remember and call it to mind.

It continues with verse:14 and 15, "you are the light of the world. A city that is set on a hill cannot be hidden. Nor do they light a lamp and put it under a basket, but on a lampstand and it gives light to all who are in the house." This is why I have loved to teach my God's word all these years, because I could see it illuminating those He sent me to.

Having realized that my purpose in this live is to love God and be His light by using the love letter He wrote to His children. Only He knows my time to come home, so I ask Him to let me be a vessel through whom He can pour this living water. As He says so powerful in Hebrews 10:14, "For by one offering He has perfected forever those who are sanctified.

TO GOD BE ALL THE HONOR AND GLORY

Ever since my Savior redeemed me, and I was sure of my forgiveness, I longed to be with Him. Agreeing with Paul in one thing however, how he put it in Philippians 1:21 "For me to live is Christ, and to die is gain. However, he continues in verse :23 for I am hard-pressed between the two, having a desire to depart and be with Christ, which is far better. And then he says in verse :24 "nevertheless, to remain in the flesh is more needful for you."

So, I agree with Paul, and even though my own four children were already saved, there were still the rest of my family. Getting to work by bringing them before my Savior daily, gave me great hope. Sad to say, most of my family told me not to bring my God into their home and not to tell them about Him until eight years later. Suddenly they began to have questions about Him and then listened to the Salvation plan.

Finally they came into the kingdom and were one by one baptized and attended my church. When my stubborn little mom, being the last, got baptized, I thanked my God in tears. Satan will do whatever he can to take praise and glory away from God. That is why, I make absolutely sure that I do not take credit for what my God does through me.

He has always supplied all the needs for my children and I, as well as all those I prayed for unless we abused what He provided. Being greatly encouraged by my Creator's wonderful promises, and the stories of His feeding so many, I never worried. Philippians 4:19 assures me "And my God supplies all my needs according to His riches in glory by Christ Jesus."

It would have been an insult to Him if I would have been concerned for them, unless there was an emergency. This beloved God I follow has such wonderful and encouraging promises in the letter He wrote to His children. Another of my favorite Scriptures is Isaiah 40:29 where he says, "He gives power to the week and to those who have no might, He increases strength."

Then in verse :31 "But those who wait on the Lord will renew their strength, they shall mount up with wings like eagles, they shall run and not be weary, they shall walk and not faint. Oh, praise this awesome God of love.

THE BATTLES ARE THE LORD'S AND SO ARE THE MIRACLES

Renewing my strength and mounting up like eagles was a strong desire suddenly, because I longed to be a better servant to my God. I prayed for some closer interaction with this precious Savior so I would be able to teach His word with greater knowledge. I loved that my Lord is immutable, which means that He can and will never change, this means I do not ever have to worry that He might change His mind about me.

My favorite of our miracles is the one of my great grandchild Kayla, which I raised for six years. She was eight now and like all the rest of them she loved fishing, so five of us went to lake Gregory. At one end of the lake was a big wall where the water was packed thick with seaweed. Explaining to the tree girls not to go near it because if they fell in, it would be impossible for them to swim out or anyone to come and rescue them.

I helped them realize that the seaweed would be tangling around their feet making it impossible to move. It looked like they agreed and went off fishing with my oldest daughter. Earlier that afternoon my Kayla had given a tiny old lady, sitting on a side bench, one of the witnessing booklets we always pass out. I just had a foot injury, so I stayed in my chair and worked on a report, while they were fishing.

After about two hours, the four fisher-ladies returned and my daughter decided to go home with her girls, this left only Kayla and me at that side of the lake. While I was packing up our stuff, my girl was still standing by the lake, about seven feet from my car. Coming out from behind my car I heard a small yipe, and Kayla was gone.

Realizing she had fallen into the lake, I ran as fast as I could, realizing that my arms, even though long, would never be able to reach her. Calling out to our Savior, I laid down and saw my girl far down, but not in the water. She had landed, not in the water but on a small circle of gravel. She was still too far below for me to bring her up.

I looked around but no one was left, everyone had gone home because it was Sunday evening. Suddenly, that little lady from the bench next to me, reached down and brought Kayla up in two seconds. I could not believe it because she was so much shorter than me, it should have been impossible for her arm to reach Kayla.

My girl and I hugged and when we turned our faces to thank her, there was no one, not one person in that large parking lot or beach. My sweet girl and I cried and hugged again and before we could speak, we knew it had been Kayla's angel and we thanked our beloved God for sending her. We both looked down and saw that the fishing pole had drifted off a little, however that small pile of gravel she had landed on was gone. All of our family thanked this gracious Lord, and we will never forget His miracle.

One of the other miracles was my car accident in Kentucky. A family friend and I had gone out to have lunch and share the

Lord's work in our life this past year. Having prayed for everyone a while we headed home. We had just pulled into my son's driveway, when there was this horrible noise and impact. A car had come off the street, went through the yard and crashed full force into the passenger side, where I was located.

There was an enormous pain on my right, I was crushed in my seat and covered with thousands of small pieces of glass. To make a long story short, my son Bill's fire partners pealed me out of my friend's car seat. This was Bill's day off, but he was notified instantly and his partners told him if that young lady had hit the car one more foot to the front, I would not be alive because of where it would have impacted me.

After two months in the hospital, while my cracked bones were growing back together and my pelvis healed, I was released. Having been told that walking again would not be a possibility, I stayed with my son another two weeks and headed back to California. Two weeks later I began to walk and am whole now. For the second miracle, with the surprise of a settlement, I was able to pay off my home, my car and the only loan I had.

I AM EXACTLY WHERE MY SAVIOR WANTS ME

Praising my Lord over everything, no matter how small, has become a joy to me because I feel it honors this powerful God. He has increased my faith and I enjoy my times with Him more than ever, waiting to hear His precious voice. If I desire something big and wonder if I can do something for it, my beloved God brings up Zechariah 4:6 where He says to Zerubbabel "Not by might nor by power, but by My Spirit." Well, I got the message and let Him work.

Being where He wants me, lets me relax and use what my Creator has given me and am able to say "Thank You" more often to Him. This wonderful God enjoys the small thank you's and the small prayers as much as the big ones. One of my loved stories is the prayer of Jabez and I said it often, "Oh that You would bless me indeed, and enlarge my territory, that Your hand would be with me, and that You would keep me from evil, that I may not cause pain."

This prayer I said daily especially the 35 years I volunteered in The Youth Detention Center, because I wanted my Lord to give me more days in there. He answered that prayers and, I was allowed two extra evenings. Because my job with Campus Crusade was in the daytime, all my personal ministries had to be evenings and weekends. I know with my whole heart that my daily prayers for my family will be answered also.

Having made sure that they said the Salvation prayer and most of them got baptized, but not all are living by His wonderful instructions. By lifting them up before their Savior however, I believe strongly that His hands are on them always. This helps me never to give up and there are times that He lets me see glimmers of light in their lives. This is why the story of being salt and light is so valuable to me because I want to be this in their lives.

NO WEAPON FORMED AGAINST ME SHALL PROSPER

Having shared with you in my first book the beautiful comfort my beloved Savior gave me, and how He told me that He is my husband now, lets me add to this. It has been 48 years since He gave me this promise and the pain and loneliness diminished. Even the put down and criticism by others became less important.

After my daughters were married, there were only my sons and I, and three years later, we moved to the local mountains. Becoming Christians made raising my boys so much easier and it affected my daughters also. Our lives changed so much that the rest of our family noticed and began to seek this awesome, loving God as well.

However, at times of slipping back into the old self, we knew now Who to run to for help and believed that perfection is coming. That is always the true answer, knowing where the only help lies and not listening to others or the enemy.

There is a true and powerful help in 2 Corinthians 10:3 and :4. saying "For though we walk in the flesh, we do not war according to the flesh. For the weapons of our warfare are not carnal, but mighty in God, for pulling down strongholds." This brings my thoughts into captivity to the obedience of my Savior, and I can depend on His help.

Again, running to His book is always the best answer to any situation especially when the suggestion comes from the enemy. The answer comes as always from the Savior and He says in John 15:3 "you are already clean because of the word which I have spoken to you," He continues in verse :4, "Abide in Me and I in you. As the branch cannot bear fruit of itself, unless it abides in the vine, neither can you unless you abide in Me."

I know I use John 15 much, but I cannot think of anything more powerful whenever I tried making something work without Him. When my beloved Savior says in John 14:6 "I am the way, the truth and the life" gives me all the answer I need whenever someone says, oh yeah? Where do you get this from?

I get this from the only One who made this Christian life and the eternal life possible, the One who saved me. And as Jesus was leaving this earth, He promised to send us another Helper in John 14:16 and :17"And I will pray the Father and He will give you another Helper that He may abide with you forever, the Spirit of truth."

ALL TRIALS ARE TEMPORARY

Having been through some of those trials, the answer was always in the words of my beloved God. I could never explain all of them, however my testimony would be in the before Christ and the after Salvation.

There is such an encouragement in 1 Peter 4:12 where he says "Beloved, do not think it strange concerning the fiery trial, which is to try you, as though some strange thing is happening to you, but rejoice to the e xtend, that you partake of Christs sufferings, that when His glory is revealed, you may also be glad about exceeding joy."

Knowing this beautiful Scripture would have helped greatly when it was my turn for a fiery trial. But even then, my not knowing it helps me realize that my Savior was present even then. Peter continues in verse :14, "If you are approached for the name of Christ, blessed are you, for the Spirit of glory and of God rests on you."

On their part He is blasphemed, but on your part, He is glorified." So, never forget, that all trials are temporary. Keep remembering the wonderful ending of our Saviors book. I will continue to write to you, till my Father says "this is all",

with love and prayers, HANNAH